BOOK BENCHERS
PUBLICATIONS
PRESENTS

THE DREADFUL LAND

Compiled By

BERDHISHA P

&

DHARSHINI M

AELAY PUBLICATION

A dream come true for every writers out there. We spot every possible problem for the writers, help in rectifying them and guide them towards the best outcome. We make sure to understand your needs, dreams and expectations, and nourish them with our services and stop not until we fulfill your dreams. The writers have a right and freedom to choose what they want here. They have us to guide them through the hardest path until the end. Believe in us.

Aelay Publication - by a writer for the writers.

BOOK BENCHERS

Book Benchers is the affiliate of Aelay publication. Both the publication is handled by Astro.
Aelay plays the role of publishing solo books.
And Book Benchers is epically for publishing anthologies.

Book Benchers have 2 different teams.
1. Tamil

2. English/Hindi

Never mind what our main motive is to help all the budding writers, who are seeking for their dream of publishing their own book to come true.

We are there to help out everyone.
In guiding for starting up with your carrier in compiling until finishing up your full book.

<u>COPYRIGHT</u>

First Edition: October 2021

Design And Executed by

ISBN : 978-93-91423-87-2
Page : 128

ACKNOWLEDGEMENT

To list who all have helped us is difficult because they are so numerous and the depth is so enormous. We would like to acknowledge the following as being idealistic channels and fresh dimensions in the completion of this book.

We take this opportunity to thank the Co-authors for being a part of this book and submitting their beautiful writer-ups and making this book more special.

We would like to thank the publication team for providing the necessary facilities required for the completion of this book. We take this opportunity to thank our book editor for the moral support and guidance.

Lastly, We would like to thank every person who directly or indirectly helped me in the completion of the book especially my parents and peers who supported me throughout my book.

<u>DISCLAIMER</u>

This Anthology is a work of fiction. Our editors have tried their best to avoid any sort of plagiarism and the proof-readers have done their job of proofreading best on their part to expertise the book with unplagiarized and original content. Still if any appropriation detected, the editorial team is no where responsible, the author is solely responsible for such acts. We have well guided our co-authors to submit their original write-ups.

FOUNDER

IRUDAGA ASTRO

Irudaga Astro, From Tirunelveli, Founder of
Aelay and BB (Book Benchers)
He had completed his BE.
He has written 3 Tamil poetry book's which
hits the top list on social media!
His main aim is to allow the writers to
publish their words as their book rather than
just Posting them on Insta.

LINK AND POSTER MAKER

CATHERINE ASMI T

Catherine Asmi T, From Tirunelveli
She has completed her M.com
Her passion is Drawing and Designing.

TEAM HEAD

She is a passionate writer from Chennai. Writing makes her pressure go away. She had played the role of co-author for more than 100+ Antho's.
She would like to thank her parents and her Loveable Brother for supporting her rather than stopping her from what she wanted to do! For being the main reason for achieving her dreams. As well as for standing beside her in all the ups and downs. Whenever she feels like she needs to get out of her stressful timing or feels like she needs peacefulness, she starts to paint, she would never mind sitting in the same place for so many hours when it comes to her painting. She believes that anyone could hurt her, But never her books could!!

Catch her in Insta and FB
Insta: @theinnocentheart
FB: KA. PARINASRI

BERDHISHA P (COMPILER)

Berdhisha, born and bought up in Kaniyakumari District, Tamil Nadu. For her, it's a heaven with beautiful nature. Now she was settled down in Coimbatore, Tamil Nadu. She completed her Master's Degree in Coimbatore. She is a poet who loves to share her own thoughts and imagination, which has its own uniqueness. She manifests the beauty of nature in her poems. Furthermore, she loves to write and read novels. She is a blogger, you can read her poems in http://berdhisha96.blogspot.com/. She is a Co-author for about 80+ Anthologies and compiling 6 Anthologies. Her first published Anthology is "The Universal Mind". She loves nature, which is her best friend and also she loves to travel in order to enjoy the nature's fresh breeze with her beloved one.

Insta Id : thoughts_of_mine_the_muse

WHEN HORROR HITS

In the midst of the night

She was walking alone

She was busy on thinking something

Lose her way by that.

Suddenly she recognized

She was in the midst of forest

Only darkness was with her,

She gets panic

Her heart beats fast

And sounds like drums

Sweat washes her body

Legs started to shiver.

She felt someone was there

A black magic woman

Spells something

She follows that black woman.

The black woman

Cut her neck with a sword

Blood flashes like spray

Black woman immolate her.

She got more powers

THE DREADFUL LAND

She become more vigorous

She turned as a beast

She howled and roared in hunger.

Went to a village,

She killed all men and drank their blood

She killed all women and ate their flesh

She immolated all children for dark devil.

Suddenly that girl

Screamed loudly

Opened her eyes,

It was just her hallucination.

When horror hits

Our extreme level of imagination

Flows as visuals

With horrific effect.

DHARSHINI M (CO-COMPILER)

She is Dharshini .M from Tamilnadu. She is scholar, completed Masters in English literature. She has huge passion on writing. She is friendly, supportive and energetic young soul. Her friends calls as her as Dharshji. She believe that optimistic thoughts will ensure to lead a great life and wants to spread it through her words that she scribe. She always carries a hope that she will shine soon in her passion. She has participated in many anthologies and she is also successful doing quite few projects as complier. She has also published a solo book named 'Vox of mine '.

MY HORROR EXPERIENCE

At the time of my Schooling during annual leave. We always went to my grandma's home in a village. After few days my parents will back to our home leaving me in her house to spend the vacation with my grandparents. I have a set of mischievous friends over there. We always had done my experiment things for creating memories and fun. One day, we plan to go to graveyard which is located far away from the village. As it was village everyone slept before 8'o clock. At once my grandparents slept. My friends and I were ready to go there. We had taken torch lights in our hands and on the way to the graveyard. We heard many mysterious sounds and have an intuition that some follows us. We afraid a lot and in that place the dogs barking sound were in an extreme level. It's very scary to go into the darkness. One among my friend has cried to go back to home. As we are small age one. We also scared a lot and run away from the place after hearing scary sounds as a racer. It's quite funny while thinking now and scary too.

LIST OF CO-AUTHORS:

1. Kalamkaar

2. Jebisha

3. Mydeensha

4. Priya Singh

5. Mohammed Niyaz

6. M. Srinithi

7. Srija Sadhukhan

8. Lipsa Dabhi

9. Harshita Verma

10. Aarushi Giria

11. Juliet Hudait

12. S. Harshana

13. Aswin S A

14. Tasneem Sheikh

15. Debangana Dutta

16. Nirudhi N. R

17. R. Jeeva Latha

18. M. Gayathri

19. Sheikh Adnaan Afridi

20. M.Aiswarya

21. Asbhin Diana P

22. E.Arun Gnana Mozhi

23. Har Deepansh Bahadur Sinha

24. Oviya sakthivel

25. Deesha soni

26. Kevin Pavithren. J

27. Agrima Viraj

28. Pandeeswari.M

29. N. Dharsshini.

30. Shalini.B.S

31. Mohana priya.S.K

32. Kajal Chaudhary

33. Talima Das

34. P. Sangareshwari

35. Aditi Singh

36. Banupriya.K

37. Debanjali Adhikary

38. Smita G Naidu

39. Deepalakshmi. S

40. Sakthi Vel P

41. Balasivanethri Ganesan

42. Pragati Giri

43. Naveen bhardwaj

44. Durga Balamadhavan

45. Krishnapriya

46. Kaarthikvel.V.S

47. Keerthana

48. Abhinav Agarwal

49. Muthu Vinnarasi M

50. I. K. Hemilaa

KALAMKAAR

This is Kalamkaar. He is from Uttrakhand bought up in Meerut(Up). His hobbies are reading and writing. His interest is in writing. He love writing. He is part of 600+Anthologies as Co-Author. He won 640+ Certificate in Writing, He Start writing 28 February 2020. He is part of 20+ anthology as Co Author going for record and He is omg record holder as Co -Author of Book Called Laposia. He is simple and people observer. His insta handle is kalamkaar51 and e-mail kalamkaar51@gmail.com. He believes in Karma.

Insta id: Kalamkaar51

HAUNTED ROOM

I had a summer vacation. I told to my father lets visit somewhere. My dad says ok then let's go to Nainital. Next day we went to Nainital. We all reached nainital, We booked 3 rooms in advance. We had dinner, we went to sleep in our room. I got to the sound of fighting Like Husband Wife Fighting I was asleep. When i got out of the room no one was there. As I come out everyone is silent. I saw no one around. This happened to me the next night, this time the baby was also crying. I went out baby silent, laughing out loud. Went a little, the voice of the woman's cry came, I started to know where the waiter gave the voice, sir, where are you going. Waiter said to me Where are the sounds of crying i did not listen then I back to room. I hear a voice came to me help me i was alone. Then the next morning I told the waiter all and asked him the truth. When i gave pressure to the waiter, A family committed suicide in the room next to you. Where did i take me there now, Let's see who are there. There was no one in the room we went to, then we came out from there, so the room was left open with the waiter because his boss called him. I woke up and hear the voice of crying, and my family was asleep in the room. Went to the next room from which the voice was coming. There the lady in the room was sitting in a slip, and her long hair scary face and eyes were white. Seeing her, I screamed mummy and fainted and my family came quickly and took me away. The next day we left for home from Nainital.

JEBISHA

Jebisha, a Journalism Student. She writes poems and articles that speaks about the social issues. Writing is my Passion. She is working as a co-author in more than thirty anthologies.

Insta id : @jebisha.jebisha.5680

THE SCARS OF MY PEOPLE

That day and nights were scary. They are not refugees. They are the aborigines of the land treated as refugees. They had been raising their voice for their rights from 80's. They are the normal people with beautiful hearts. They became warriors when most of them were killed and their self respect was not considered by some culprits. They were not terrorists, they were the warriors with loyalty and purity in hearts. The one and only soldiers in the history who made rules not to intake drinks. They fight for their rights and still fighting to survive. It is not a great triumph to the culprits who defeated a race with the help of nineteen nations. They protests and fights for their dignity and rights. Women and girls were abused and killed. The world wide countries now started to speak about the war that destroyed a race. After twelve years, some countries speaks for the justice for genocide. They were not alive now, but their history speaks their pains. The scars of the aborigines. Still raising the voice for their rights in their lands. It's not a fantasy or a story to move on. These are the scars of Eelam..

MYDEENSHA

He is Mydeensha. He is an hard working person. He loves to write his thoughts and love on his beloved love. He writes to impress her and wanna make her to feel Special and loved

Insta id: Yuvisha 12

MY HORROR EXPERIENCE

I have set of gang whom are mischievous and jovial beings. One night, we stayed in one of my friend's home. We are held in the upstairs. Dancing, singing, chatting and mocking each others. The time may be around 1.30 to 2 am. Deep dark and calmness spread everywhere. As we felt sleepy, we getting ready to make our bed. Suddenly we heard a huge loud in the opposite side. We rushed there in thought of a thief. We are on the flash light and seem nobody there. As soon we feel someone throw sand under our foot. We are totally scared, and heard weird voices. Everyone shouted, it takes few more minutes to make us calm. Everyone face is filled with scare. By hearing the sound his parents came and ask to sleep well. Then, we realises there no sand under our foot. It's still misery how we all feel the hit of the sand under our foot while there is nothing. It repeats every Friday night and we are experience the thrill for fewer times.

PRIYA SINGH

Priya Singh is born & brought up in Dewas, MadhyaPradesh. She's completed Masters of Computer Science. She is a Former Educationist, communication Trainer. She's the Co-Author of the Anthologies:- "It's all about two phase : love & hate" ,"Words From Heart", "Fierce, Fearless N Flawed" & "In the way of borehole". All are available in Amazon. Till today, She's worked in 150+ Anthologies as a Co-Author. Her writing keeps her at ease. She mostly write quotes on thoughts. She loves inspiring young minds.

Insta id: instant__thoughts

SCARY QUOTES

Cursed Twins; they live together,

When one appears another disappears,

They can listen each-other

But can't see & mutually talk,

Cursed they are!!

Trying to connect a friend on call,

He appears without recall, seems weird though,

I asked about his appearance,

Responded "Think of devil & he appears",

His mother was informed his demise.

In gloomy days of summers,

We saw something hanging on the tree,

When we went close, it had flown by.

Sitting alone on terrace at night,

Heard a weird sigh,

Saying be with me till I'm alive,

Soul knew It was nothing just a sight.

MOHAMMED NIYAZ

Mohammed Niyaz hails from Mumbai - The City Of Dreams. He often loves to write poetries and short music video stories for his own youtube channel. Apart from this Mohammed is currently working on his upcoming anthologies, as well writing poetries since 2013. You can find him on facebook/mohammed niyaz as well on instagram @niyazsks.

Insta id : niyazsks

FEAR OF DEATH

With tolls increasing day by day.

We are hereby near to an inch for our last way.

The sudden change of the situation.

Has taken away breathe taking conditions.

Being normal now is like a wish come true.

If we stay for a while till and until few.

The entire world is now caused by an invisible
disease.

Which can be possibly happens to anyone with
ease.

The almighty's judgement is yet to take place.

On the day of resurrection with pace.

Crises of poverty, economic fall is the new era.

We can see how helpless all of us became since
every criteria.

Now or never is the on going myth.

Together we experienced the "fear of death".

M. SRINITHI

She is srinithi. She completed her master degree in English literature. She is a blogger and budding writer who written many excellent blogs and verse. She is outstanding scholar and talented woman.

Insta id : Srinithi_manoharan

FEARFUL NIGHT

It was night time when I return from a movie. The dog was barking after it Saw me. This is the usual way I used to go out. I get fear why this dog bark while seeing me. Suddenly every dog in the nearby Street started barking. Fear started inside me second by second. I reach the lane of my home. I am ready to get a key from a secret place. I insert a hand behind the photo which in front of the house to get a key. Suddenly lizard came outside. After that I having fear of getting a key. Everyone was sleeping in the room. So I took my phone to call my mom to open the door. My palm is full of sweating. The phone fell from my hand. So I bow to take the phone. Suddenly a shadow crossed me. A drop of sweating from my forehead fell. I called my mom and she opened the door. Behind her, I went inside. After she went inside I saw a shadow in front of me. With tons of fear, I went inside. In bed, I thought about the two shadows. In the morning went outside with a cup of coffee. Then only I realise there was a mirror on the doorstep, my shadow only reflect in the mirror. Then having thought of shadow crossed in front of the photo. Don't have an idea about it. Still, it's a mystery to me.

SRIJA SADHUKHAN

Srija Sadhukhan is 19 years old girl studying BSc Biotechnology in Amity University Kolkata. Love to write poetry and a book worm too.

Insta id: Syncopatemysuccess

GRUSEL

Locked in emptiness, looking for bliss

No one is here - darkness is everywhere,

Living with fears haunting dark thoughts

Thinking about face turned without body

Legs walked in opposite direction,

That cursed moving chair crawling alone.

I love visiting the crematorium

Haunting the part of mine that has died,

Building the biggest crematorium around.

In night screeching wooden floor

Living with ghost, enjoy haunting dead self,

Roaming aimlessly on lonely streets of necropolis.

LIPSA DABHI

She is Author and also good Co-Author. She is eighteen years old, she is student of the computer engineering. She is extraordinary person. She is always good leader. Her mam mrunal prajapati is her inspiration person and also her motivater, her friend chetna raval also supported to her and her mom manisha ben and her father nilesh bhai also supported to her for anytype of her creativity. she also wrote poems, short stories, shayries. Her writing skills almost very well and her creative collections are always best.

Insta id: __lipsa__dabhi__0829

THE DREADFUL LAND

This land is full of economics, horror and some
grateful land,

Small creatures and lots of happiness,

But sometimes shadow of horror crimes,

It's not good way.

Horror think is best but

Sometimes horror acting it's not good,

This land is I think not good now,

Because of some problems related to land.

This dreadful land stay with some good views,

Behind that it's not good land,

Stay always and connected with positivity,

Good vibes only this is best way for this land.

HARSHITA VERMA

Co-author Harshita Verma is a writer from Lucknow. She has completed her graduation in commerce stream. She has been writing poetry for the last few years as her passion. She wants to be a novelist in future.

Insta id: 0___hsh

YOU

Walking in the distance I saw you

Whom I had lost three years ago.

The same features the same smile

You were gone but you are here again

As I walk towards you in curiosity

I notice changed features like after the accident
and a grin

You are not you but a bad dream

As I near you I realise what walking towards hell
fell like

At last I reach you and I know this is not the end

You will continue to haunt me forever

As you are here for me.

AARUSHI GIRIA

This is Aarushi Giria, a 16 year old poet who has a perspective which she doesn't refrain from sharing with the world. Finds joy in smelling new books, the feeling of wind in the hair and barely taking 10 to make a poem. That being said, she's also just a teen using her passion to be vocal.

Insta id : verse.ion

WHAT SCARES ME?

Deep sleep had engulfed me,

My eyes were full of sleep, nothing I could see.

It was a very long day,

I had an exam, what else should I say.

I went straight to my bedroom,

I slept pretty soon.

I don't know how much time had passed,

When I woke up aghast.

I could swear I heard a noise,

I thought it was the neighbourhood boys.

I ignored them and tried sleep again,

But came the voice again, representing that of some
men.

I started feeling scared,

To get up and walk down the stairs, I dared.

As I walked out, the door behind me shut,

And on my hand, I noticed a cut.

I knew it was something unusual, I couldn't tell what,

Just then under the door my leg got caught.

THE DREADFUL LAND

I

shouted in pain and wishes someone could come,

The very next moment my leg got released, and I
felt numb.

I heard a loud thud from the kitchen.

And then from the den.

What unholy thing my house possessed?

Was someone taking my test?

I hid underneath the center table,

To speak even one word, I was unable.

I don't know when I slept again,

But when I woke up, I saw my friends surrounding
me.

Along with them, there was also a comedian.

In the middle of all this, I forgot it was my
birthday,

To surprise me, they used this way.

Tears of both happiness and fear started flowing
down my eyes,

I wish they would have acted a little more wise.

JULIET HUDAIT

She is Juliet, Currently studying in Grade 10 of Anthony Claret School ICSE. From West Bengal and Currently at Bangalore. Photography and Writing are her favourites! Co-authored 50+ books and Compiling 3. A Bibliophile and an Astrophile.

Insta id: @juliethudait

ROSE OR ROSALIA?

Alex was a 20 year old Medical student. He was fair, handsome and had blonde hair. He was the smartest among the guys in his college. He had been approached by many girls at college but he accepted none. He was in love with a girl named Rosalia, who he cheated on. She commit suicide soon after. He was then in a relationship with Olivia who again cheated on him. That's when he decided never to fall in love again but that decision only lasted till a girl named Rose joined the college. Rose was fair and cute like a Disney princess. On her first day she spoke to him as soon as she enters. They become pretty good friends. A month passes by and they were getting pretty close to each other. One day Rose invited Alex to the woodland beside a stream to spend a night camp together. Rose said Alex to reach the destination by 7 p.m. She also added that she would be there before him. Alex entered the woodland to get past it and reach the bank of the stream. There was a strong wind and the trees made eerie sounds. Alex took out his torch and continued walking. Suddenly his torch started flickering. Alex thought that the batteries were down and he continued walking. When he reached the end of the woodland, he found the camp but there was no sign or Rose. He bent down and pointed his torch inside the tent to check if she's there. When the flickering light fell on the body, it was not Rose. It was Rosalia! The girl he cheated on 5 years back. She just looked uglier with tattered clothes, red eyes and a mouth full of blood. Alex shouted out loud but Rosalia choked him to death. That's when her soul rested in peace

HARSHANADEVI. S

Harshanadevi from Ramanathapuram, Tamilnadu, pursing my master's. She is interested in writing and trying to explore something new.

Insta id: _queen_fa_ma_king

NEW FRIEND

Is really dark scary?

I don't think so

Dark are our another friend

Dark gave us new friends

With long teeth,

Wearing white dress

They can fly,

Face full of scar,

Blood strains in their body,

Odour when they cross us

Because they don't take shower

They wear same dress for many years

That's the reason
Yes! It's little bit scary.

ASWIN S A

Aswin S.A. is a budding writer. He writes in various themes exploring the true meaning of existence, connecting literature with various aspects of love and life. He writes his poems with extreme passion and all his words are filled with rhyming vividness. There is so much to learn about life from his inspiring lines. I've known him personally and he is such a person with uniqueness as his lines. Do read the lines and enjoy for yourselves.

Insta id : let_me_write_something__

ALL HAIL

Hail Macbeth!

Hail Hamlet!

Hail Othello!

All hail the legends

Of what makes myself

To raise my eye brows.

Melancholic Hamlet with

Knowledge like a beast.

Brave Macbeth with

Selfish political desire.

Strongest Othello with

Fame and Jealousy.

Horror it was!

Horrible it is!

Halloween to be!

Told, untold, foretold;

The pearls of wisdom

Wrinkles in an evil Man,

Sparkles in a good Man.

For flesh- Death is the destiny of

Good and Bad.

For soul- Death is the entry of

Good and Bad.

TASNEEM SHEIKH

Tasneem Sheikh of Assam, author of **'Tulips Coffee and You'**, is a 17 year old poet and writer, co-author of 80 anthologies and numerous magazines. She was recognized as a young achiever in English Literature by esteemed personalities of Maria's Montessori in 2016. A critic, counsellor and humanitarian, apart from her endearment for literature, she also holds a passion towards music, expressive artwork, creativity and adventures.

Insta id : la_nuit_portrait

BEWITCHED

I've looked under my bed,

I've looked into the dark woods.

I've seen eyes bloody red,

Claws sharp when night crawls in.

I've seen monstrous figures, huge and

Noises eerie, fading into the dark,

But that's not what I've been looking for.

I wonder if throughout all this time,

The demon has been me.

And once into the twilight I went

Running through the bridge across the swamp,

Into the forbidden hill, near the sorcerer's potion
pot.

And the evil aura dragged me to a few drops

And I see myself turning into a witch.

DEBANGANA DUTTA

She is Debangana Dutta,daughter of Mitali and Dipankar Dutta. Right now, she is studying in Class 12. It was very early in her life when she realized writing is her true passion and since then she haven't looked back. Her pen has been her constant companion, in times both good and bad. She is a logophile in the true sense of the word, and she sincerely hope her honest passion would be reflected in her work. She is very pleased to be in this world of Anthology and it would give her immense joy if her writings bring solace to all the people out there. According to her, writing isn't a work or job, it's the most genuine form of expressing what we actually feel. A book is a dream we hold in our hands. She want to let this dream create her own reality.

Insta id: @_._bubble_poetry_._

NIGHTMARE

Not all nightmares scare us but there are few nightmares that teach us an important part. Shreya, a forensic expert, that day when entered her lab seemed in deep thoughts. Her friend Neha asked her the reason of her confused thoughts. The story narrated by Shreya, left Neha stunted. Last night when I was sleeping I heard someone digging in my yard. I got up and peeped out of the window but could not find anything. Just considered it as my exhaustion, went back to sleep. Few moments later heard the shower flowing in my bathroom. When I went to check, I saw the bathroom floor covered with mud. This freaked me out a bit. I also smell some wet sand from my cupboard. With my fast heart beats when I moved closer to my cupboard and opened it, all my clothes and cupboard were muddy. That was such a dreadful moment for me. I ran towards my phone to call someone for help. When I dialed the number I could hear the digging sound in the phone. The phone was scaring me more. I ran out of my house for some help, but, as I reached my yard I saw a man covered in mud in front of me. He asked me to follow him to the world of zombies as in the path of worldly happiness I have killed the child inside me. I was just breathing as a body but not living as a soul. Being alive from body, but, dead from inside is a zombie trait. Just like the zombie craves for blood and not life, human too craves for success and not happiness. The muddy man pushed me into the damp mud pool. With the fear of losing my life, I woke up and realized it all to be a dream. I could still smell mud all around me and the smell kept me reminding something the zombie dream had taught me. I was realizing the real value of staying happy. People sleep and get nightmare, I had woken up to it.

NIRUNDHI N.R

Nirudhi N.R is an English Student. She is enchanting about writing poems and quotes. She has been a co-author of more than fifty anthologies. She wants to become a writer in the upcoming future. She is happy to be a part of this incredible book.

Insta id: bae_niru

THEY NEVER SEE

I am the one that stows away under your bed,

I wake in obscurity, and I lay down with the dead,

I am the one you hear call unto you yet attempt

As you would you won't ever see me,

I am the eyes in your storeroom every evening.

I stand by in the shadows concealed by the light,

I am the strides that stroll past your entryway,

The scratch on your windows, the squeak in your
floor,

I watch you in sleep, I take in your ear;

I say to you things that you don't wish to hear,

For I am the, never see, the seller of death,

And I live in your bad dreams until your perishing
breath.

R. JEEVA LATHA

She was a positive spreader through her writings. Her name is R.Jeeva latha. Studying M.Sc physics I year.

Insta id: meow_lubb510

DREADFUL LAND

What's actually dreadful land?

She heard the sound

That was so occult

It darkening her eyes

Thinks goes on her mind

Is ghost are real?

The door was knocked

Her skin gets goose bumps

She opens her eyes

She saw her mom

OMG she was dreaming

So only her eyes

Gets darkened....

M.GAYATHRI

She is Mrs.Gayathri, who has completed her Master degree in English Literature. She has started her writings recently and she has written few anthologies as a co-author. She is a budding writer.

Insta id: ramgayathri3

A DREADFUL LAND

A girl named Tabitha goes to college for her higher studies where she stays in a hostel in the college. She gets some friends there. One of the habits of Tabitha is that she has been interested in watching movies since her childhood but she used to watch only horror movies. When she comes to the hostel after college, she starts watching movies at night. She invites her friends with her but her friends refuse to watch the movie. Then she alone starts watching that movie. A few days passed and suddenly one day a man began to follow her. Seeing when Tabitha is alone the man will try to mislead her But Tabitha will somehow escape from that situation. But one day the man make Tabitha faint and take her to his house and spoil her. But Tabitha is reluctant to tell this to others so she does not tell it to anyone. One day as usual while she was watching a movie she had a dream. In DREAM... Tabitha and her friends had gone to a forest then suddenly Tabitha saw a small child there and she goes towards that little child. So her friends and she will part in a different direction. That child suddenly disappears when Tabitha chases the child but she continues to follow the child. Her friends are looking for her on one hand. But they can't find her so they go to their college hostel. In college whoever asked about Tabitha they managed to say that Tabitha has gone out for the research of her project. In REAL.... Now Tabitha has become conscious then she realizes it is her dream. Then after two days her friends plan to go out to enjoy their weekend.

So, they went to one forest. Tabitha gets shocked by seeing that forest because the forest is exactly look like which comes in her dream. She is very nervous...Then all the events she dreamed of actually happened now. A few days go by and she returns to the hostel a week later. Her friends are very happy to see her but she behaves very differently. When she sees her figure in the mirror her figure is not visible in that mirror she tries to tell it to her friends but when her friends come and see her figure is visible. She is very confused because she has no recollected what happened in forest, in dreams and in reality. So one day while she was watching the movie as usual a ghost appeared on the screen. Tabitha is shocked to see the ghost because that Ghost is in the image of the little child she saw in the forest. Now the demon tells the Tabitha what happened in that forest. As Tabitha chases after her, the demon child makes Tabitha faint and enters into her body. Now Tabitha asks the ghost child why you entered into my body. Then Ghost child explains Tabitha about what happens in its life. Before 3 years while that child went to that forest with her family she was lost in that forest. Her parents searched that child everywhere. In that forest the child was suffering at the peak of fear..The baby's heart began to beat faster...At that time a man came there but he misbehaved with the child without trying to save her and after a while the child died...Now the ghost child shows the image of the man on the screen. The demon child told that I should take revenge on that man and that is why I was entered inside your body. Tabitha accepts the demand of Ghost child because Tabitha was also spoiled by the same man who spoiled the life of the little child. So, Tabitha started following man wherever he goes and one day while he is in his house he heard a sound like (jal jal jal jal) and he heard the sound of knocking door. Then he goes to open the door but finds nobody. So he close the door and he finds that ghost child is behind him. Then after a moment ghost child killed the man. Tabitha came back to the hostel and her friends were get shocked by seeing her because Tabitha's body was covered with blood...Her Friends enquires her, what happened to her. Then that ghost child appeared infront of Tabitha's friends and explains everything... Then the ghost child went out of Tabitha's body and Tabitha becomes normal. Afterwards she leads her life happily without any disturbance... MORAL: Those who have done wrong should be punished accordingly.

SHEIKH ADNAAN AFRIDI

Sheikh Adnaan Afridi (born on 9 July 2010) is an 11 year old art enthusiast and comic writer. He resides in Guwahati, Assam, studying in Shrimanta Shankar Academy. He's greatly absorbed in science and started drawing comics from a young age. He has also bagged medals and trophies in singing and art competitions. Apart from writing stories, his hobbies include reading, travelling, cycling, gaming and watching movies.

HE FOLLOWS ME HOME

Sometimes I walk alone

Sometimes he follows me around,

When I'm lying on my bed, sleepless

I see him dancing under the dim light

In shadows.

When I go to school, he doesn't come along

But when I return,

He does welcome me home.

He says he doesn't stay under my bed

He says he's afraid too,

So instead we hold hands

And walk together.

Sometimes I walk alone

Sometimes he follows me around.

M.AISWARYA

She is Aiswarya from Tamil Nadu. She is pursuing B. Ed in teacher training and also completed Bachelor in English. She is trained teacher with good knowledge. She loves to read and shares her view of books to her friends. She now turns to budding writer.

FIRST BREATH

To relax myself I used to go night walk

But that day not like usual

Several interference was there in inner and
exterior

Suddenly I listen my inner voice "RUN OFF"

Instantly heard unguessed voice from outward

I get away without search what was that

When it happened I got a thing of childhood
memories

Someone waiting to find them

Yeah! it is the game of hide and seek

I convinced myself like someone here near to me

I begin rapid walk to find them

But that the unguessed voice continuous

I had a terrific breath like breaking heart

At last I reached place of bright

It felt like discover someone

After that distress I take first long breath

Simple memories utilize to bring out from trouble

ASBHIN DIANA P

Asbhin Diana from Tamil Nadu. She has finished her master's in English literature from Loyola College, Chennai. She is a nature lover. She loves writing articles and poetry.

Insta id : asbhindiana

A DARK NIGHT

The lonely women hid herself behind the clouds,

Paving way for the darkness to surround,

The silence was broken by a black cat,

Whose eyes were only seen on the mat.

The girl in the home was petrified,

As she saw a shadow on her bedside,

The flickering street light and the blackness,

Inspired the shadow to be heartless.

The girl hid herself under the sheet,

To protect herself from the beast,

The ferocious shadow was set to attack,

Willing to make her its snack.

She stayed unmoved hoping to stay alive,

But what does the shadow think?

E. ARUN GNANA MOZHI

She is Arun Gnana Mozhi from Tamilnadu. She is pursuing B. Ed in teacher training and also completed Bachelor in English. She is trained teacher with good knowledge. She loves to read and shares her view of books to her friends. She now turns to budding writer.

A MYSTERIOUS NIGHT

Who they are? Where they gone in the morning? What's going inside the palace in the night?. These are the questions repeatedly rising in my mind. I usually spend my vacation in my uncle's village. On that year also my uncle picked me from the railway station. On the way, my uncle always took me to his right side while crossing the stone bridge and not allowing me to see the palace which is in the left side of that bridge. It makes more curiosity in my mind. I raised the question about that palace to my uncle. But he refused to say it. I decided to find out that mystery. So, I woke up in the night and went to the palace. While crossing the bridge, I felt that some mysteries thing happens around me. I build up my confidence and make a move. Finally, I was standing infront of the palace. I was afraid because the palace was fully decorated and people in that palace are not like normal humans. I decided to go inside the palace. But someone hold my hands and not allowing me to in. I was scared but it's none other than my uncle. He shouted me and takes me to home. Next day morning, I saw that palace it looks uglier and no one in that palace. This makes more mysterious about that palace in my mind

HAR DEEPANSH BAHADUR SINHA

He is Har Deepansh Bahadur Sinha . He belongs to Lucknow,UP. He is a research scholar of Oceanography and has done masters in Geography from National Post Graduate College. Completed his schooling from Study Hall. His hobbies are art, listening to music , cooking & loads of driving. His interest areas are Astronomy, Writing, Photography & Travelling a lot

Insta id : Deepansh_sinha

A CURSED TOWN

He was walking down the lane

Heard someone groaning in pain,

As soon as he turned around

There was a deep silence in sound.

He thought it's a hallucination

Very next second felt extreme palpitation,

Infornt of him there was a lady

She was bleeding with a dead baby.

He realized she was a ghost not a stranger

And his life was completely in danger,

Meanwhile he heard people screaming

They were shouting to run without thinking.

Unfortunately none of them survived

Since demonic spirits were revived.

OVIYA SAKTHIVEL

"Ovi Sakthi" She completed the B.Sc agriculture degree and her passion to write poems & quotes ,bharathanatiyam dancer and the best photographic skills too. Her uniqueness is to be write the quotes with "PERFECT RHYME". She had written more than 150 quotes and Poems. She is a positive vibe girl and delivers it with her smile. She wants to become a perfect author with the big support and huge response of "beautiful readers" like you all.

Insta id : ovi_sakthi_

HORROR

The aggressive night in my whole life!

Suddenly the thing fallen, was the knife

Windows shattered with sound!

Outside, some shadow walking around.

My dress rinsed with sweat;

I move from room like a jet!

My hand shivered & pressed all the switches,

The man behind me, his face full of stitches.

I shout out loud, my voice drowned!

At all of a sudden, there is nobody around;

Which made me more scared,

All the lights on, I was starred at the moment.

I closed my eyes, slept with three blankets;

I don't even move my anklet!

I wake up with jerk and thank god more;

Don't, made me to dream like this again!

DEESHA SONI

Deesha Soni..a Post Graduate and M.phil adorns the hat of a multitasker of an educationist, artist, poet, photographer, author , blogger, homemaker, wife and mother... She has 10 years experience in the field of Education as a Professor and Coordinator. Deesha has various publications to her credit ya national and international levels. Deesha has various published works to her credit... she has two books published on Amazon... named 'Just thoughts' and 'Random thoughts on pandemic'..Kindle edition and more than 100 plus published works on various online platforms. Deesha has been twice nominated for Author of a week award by Storymirror and has also won various recognitions in penning stories and write-ups.. at National and International levels... Deesha has also won many prizes in National and international levels in many write-ups... Deesha has also published her works in 235 plus anthologies of multiple genres...

Insta id : Deeshagauree

THE VAMPIRE

As Khunkhaar, the most feared vampire in the forest of Daraavnaa jungle straws blood out from the veins of his yet another victim human blood yes this Adamkhor, Vampire Khunkhaar of Daraavnaa jungle relishes every drop of brightmaroon metallic tasting human blood. Khunkhaar has blood smeared and dripping by the sides of his wide mouth... Khunkhaar then collects some blood in his black bottle and vanishes in the darkness of the jungle of Daraavnaa. Khunkhaars Bhootia Thikana is at the end of the Daraavnaa jungle where he is buried deep down under the foot of Chudail ki Pahaadi. Khunkhaar, Vampire gets to life on every Amavas by the alarm of the howling wolves. Khunkhaar has a diary surprisingly seems to be a literate vampire with the collected blood of his victim or victims he has preyed on Khunkhaar writes a new chapter with blood. This is the 200th chapter in the diary of Khunkhaar the Vampire. Khunkhaar is probably on a mission to write his biography on the victims, he has ended the games of and how is his life as a Vampire. Khunkhaar has named his book too. Vampire ki Atmakatha. Khunkhaar the Vampire didn't want to ever be a Vampire or Evil but unfortunately he became a morsel of Bargad ki Chudail. Bargad ki Chudail killed Khunkhaar, while he was a human and fed on his flesh and blood but because he was well built, skilled and brave in his life term Bargad ki Chudail turned him into a Vampire and ordered him to show his valor and wits by killing people who are hypnotically attracted to Daraavnaa jungle. It's been 100 years the story still continues with fresh blood words formed in the expressional writings of Khunkhaar though people have heard tales of Khunkhaar and Bargad ki Chudail and dread the Daraavnaa jungle yet the hypnotic scent and the melodious sound of anklets attract the passerby and grips them in spell then hunted by Khunkhaar, who feeds on the blood of people and flesh eaten by Bargad ki Chudail. While Bargad ki Chudail resides on the tree. Khunkhaar is 6 feet under. Khunkhaar has expressed his plight on his unwillingness of forcefully taking lives he stands puppet of the evil pale white Bargad ki Chudail. Ki Atmakatha book was found by some ghost hunters who found the dirty soiled blood-stained partially torn and rottenly smelly dark brown looking book whose pages were made from human flesh and stitched to bind with human hair as a thread and human bone as a needle the dreadful horrifying book expressing ki Atmakatha was lying beside a partially dug deep pit which seemed like a grave. The ghost hunters promised to release Khunkhaar from the clutches of Bargad ki Chudail. Khunkhaar Vampire told them that it was possible only when on full moon night a special iron nail empowered with holy spells would be hammered under the Bargad tree where the pale white Chudail resides. The ghost hunters then visit the Bhoothnath temple and manage to get the iron nail empowered with holy spells from the temple priest they then somehow manage to hammer it at the roots of the Bargad tree while the pale white Chudail hovers yells cries flies around in desperation creating all possible obstacles in the procedure finally when there is a final bang hammered in the iron nail. Bargad ki Chudail screams in pain Aaaaaaaaaaaaaaa!!!!!!! and vanishes forever in smoke. Khunkhaar Vampire is released from the spell and the Daraavnaa jungle becomes Suhavana Vann once again. Vampire ki Atmakatha is the weirdest book that the ghost hunters had come across in their careers. Khunkhaar the Vampire goes back in his deep grave snatching his book from the ghost hunters with mud pulled back on the grave and turned a plain ground with weeds all over it. Vampire ki Atmakatha made Khunkhaar Vampire get rid of the curse which Bargad ki Chudail had bound him with.

KEVIN PAVITHREN. J

He is Kevin Pavithren. J from Salem, Tamilnadu who finished his Under Graduation in Loyola college of arts and science Mettala. Now he is doing his Post Graduation in Government college of arts and science salem-7. He started his career as a speaker and he has participated in many speech competitions both in Tamil and English. He also participated in a photography competition and won an international certificate. He had published his poetry in Tamil and he won a state level certificate in the field of poetry. He is not only an author but also volley ball player

Insta id : urstrulykevin

THE BACK SHAD

I saw a devil,

It was so terror,

Went nearby....

Suddenly it hold my neck

Everything stopped,

But not my heartbeat.

My friend came unexpectedly,

Tried to help me!

But in vain he died by shock.

Suddenly I woke up..
Nothing it was in my dream.

AGRIMA VIRAJ

She has completed her 18 years of adventurous life living in different corners of India and is currently preparing for the competitive exam NEET. She is highly determined to pursuit her profession as a DOCTOR. The writer within her awakened when she started penning down her boundless thoughts & emotions. She has co-authored more than 50 anthologies till now. She can solemnly portray herself to the readers through her writings and express the hidden contemplations within her. Being a writer she strongly believes that the magic of words and verse can change the insight of minds and souls through rolling pens over paper. To read her poems more, follow her on Instagram: @agrima_viraj YourQuote: Agrima Viraj You can also read her blogs on: www.theuntouchedmind.wordpress.com

Insta id: @agrima_viraj

AN ORDEAL

I remember after coming back home I got
undressed

Removed my makeup and plunged over my bed so
messed

And I soon went asleep like a log without wasting
a second

Only to find myself thirsty in the late midnight of
crescent

I walked up to the fridge, took out a chilled water
bottle

It fell down on my foot so hard and made me
hobbled

I slouched to pick it up and saw some broad
footmarks

Heading towards the store room, left me dazed in
the dark

I gulped down my breath, thought it might be a
robber

I picked up a stick and forged ahead to clobber

It was silent and still and I found nobody in there

I sighed but in fear and felt an oddity in the air

I went back to sleep to hear a queer murmur of my
name

Just then I was throttled by some frosty long
fingers

I screamed liked hell and my eyes opened with
face pale

Ahh! A nightmare it was so I smiled and lingered

Felt my throat dried so went to drink cold water

And found those footmarks again on the floor

This time it was an ordeal of my courage

I froze with fear and heard the murmur again.

M.PANDEESWARI

Miss.M.Pandeeswari hails from Sattur in Virudhunagar district. She is currently pursuing second year Postgraduate English at Annamalai University. She has a keen interest in writing poetry and short stories.She has been composing the best poems since her Undergraduate College days. She has won many awards for her best poetry. She worked as a co-author in 4+ anthologies. **"யாருமில்லா தனித்தீவில்"**, **"கிராமத்துக் கண்ணகிகள்"** Were her recent poetry. Her theme is always based on Love and Nature.

BE AWARE!!!

The tiny foots entered into the darkest room. He Damned sure there was nobody. He was listened somebody's blabbering. He was able to listened a loud crying and murmuring transparently. He wish God that everything was normal and whatever he had been feel that was his hallucinations. But his fate, the same sounds were continued.

The seven years little one blinked that what happened around him. He was feel somebody's fragrance. Simply he was gone dormant mode. He can remembered his mom's words. "Be Aware...Don't enter the terrace room even without knowing...It doesn't belong to God!"

The little one's face was filled with afraid and tears. The past sounds increased frequently. He saw one dirty doll. He thrilled when he realized that doll was crying. His foots slowly move forward to the doll. The doll weep loudly. He tried to touch the doll with worst fear. The doll's bloodshed head was slowly turned. "Tom...what was I told you..you break my words!.."He stumbled and turned back. His mom stand close him. He screamed "Mommm" and she hug tightly. As turned off she noticed the words wrote by blood that "BE AWARE"!!!....

N. DHARSSHINI

She is Dharsshini. She is a College student. She writes not because she forgets, but because she overthink.

Insta id : @dharsshini_._

NIGHT PIES

Nights were her brights

light of face like moon in dark

being home busted

stepped out for a custard

Alone as always

motto to follow these days

sudden sign of a touching feel

was good enough to think it as a reel

Crappy sounds of not her walking

sassy girl wasn't stopping

A blink of her closed eyes

long breathe of her wind pipes

Ready to look at the one whose gonna make her
pies.

SHALINI.B.S

Shalini.B.S is a literature student . Her writing style are about the real feelings ,simple , understanding and joyful. She is writing under the pen name of TARA .Most of her works based on real life. she is the co-author for more 200+ books and as compiled for 5 + projects.

Insta id : Kuttyma2611

HORROR

The light from the mirror casts shadows of black,

And when I started at those shadows, the shadows started back.

The walls have ears and the

Mirror have eyes,

And they both whisper truth and lies,

They whisper to the spider and they laugh at the fly

Saying one will live and the other will die,

With screams and shouts like a pouring rain,

That comes from a place if a roaring pain.

But the walls have ears, and the mirror have eyes ,

And whether you're the fly.

ONE WILL LIVE AND THE OTHERS MUST DIE .

MOHANA PRIYA.S.K

Mohana priya.S.KS, a literature student has written many poems, quotes and short story under the pen name called "MONA". All of her works are simple, understandable and raising questions. She started writing her works at the age of 19. She is the co author for more than 200+ books and has compiled 5+ projects.

Insta id: _m_o_n_a_2719

MY HORRIBLE DREAM

When I waked up from my bed,
It fully flooded with blood....
I was freaking out,
And doesn't know the way out.....
The deep dark blood,
Makes me more scared...
I call for help and shouted,
Yet no one listened....
I am afraid to keep down my leg,
As if something might grab me....
I closed my eyes and prayed,
Suddenly a two things has fallen down,
A match box and a water suck machine,
When I light the match,
A bunch of bats were hanging in the wall....
When I use the machine, few deadly crocs were
there ....
I don't know what to do,
Suddenly water were poured on my face,
When I opened my eyes,
It's all my bloody dreams....

KAJAL CHAUDHARY

Kajal Chaudhary is a student who is currently studying in grade 12. This 17 year old girl developed a interest in poetry in 10 grade and penned up her first poem.

Insta id : @_dear_poet

WHISPER

Can you hear the whispering ?

When no one surrounds you

When you hear it

Then, turn away your ear

Don't get trauma or fear

Do not hear that whispering

When you'll do

The whispering will stop

And they will stare you

Don't ignore them

As they are not alive

They're breathe-less Dead !!

TALIMA DAS

Talima Das is a student. She has interest in writing on social media platform. She is a co-author of ten amazing anthologies.

Insta id : 1talimadas

SCARY MICRO-FICTIONS

1. He was alone and sad.

He wanted companion.

There he found companions.

They all were from the world of death.

2. His betrayal murdered her.

She comes again in his life as a nightmare.

And this nightmare becomes true.

3. He dreamed about his deceased friends every night.

The darkness of this dream woke him up.

And he made himself calm by realizing that these all were his dreams.

The friends were laughing cruelly.

He was also one of them.

P. SANGARESHWARI

She was born in the soil where Karmaveer was born. Her name is Sangareshwari. Social service activist. Many orphans and disabled children have benefited from her. And planted a lot of saplings in this community. He did his bachelor's degree in English but is more interested in Tamil. He is good at writing a lot of stories and poems. She wants to become IAS. Her strength Hope. What she often says is that one day I will definitely become an IAS officer.....

A BLOODY HALLOWEEN

Once upon a time in the little village of Lehawork
two boys were preparing their Halloween
costumes. Their names were Tom and Charles.

-I'm sure you're going to wear a mummy's
costume- said Tom.
-How do you know it?- answered Charles.
-Because you love mummies haha- laughed Tom.
-And what costume are you going to wear?
-It's a secret. You'll see it tomorrow.
The next day the two boys were excited.
Halloween was finally here! The started to
imagine all the sweets: chocolates, caramelized
apples... they could even smell them!
Night came and somebody knocked on Tom's
door. Tom went quickly to the door and opened it.
-Charles!
-Tom! You're fantastic. You costume is very cool.
Tom was wearing a Frankenstein costume.
-Let's go to recollect sweets!-shouted Tom.
-Yeah!- added Charles.
The two boys went to all the houses of the village,
knocking on their doors and saying:
"Trick or treat?" Two hours later they had a great
spat.
Suddenly Tom said: -Why don't we go to the
forest?
-No, no and a hundred times no!- shouted Charles.

THE DREADFUL LAND

-Why?
-Because I'm scared! I don't like that forest.
They discussed for a long time. Finally Tom won
and they went to the forest. When they got there
they heard a strange noise.
-What was that?-asked Charles.
-Perhaps a squirrel. Don't worry!
They came into the forest and suddenly they saw
her: a HARPY!!! A hungry harpy with their sharp
teeth and her long nails. They couldn't do
anything because the harpy fell over them. –
Nowadays, every 31st October you can hear the
cries of the two boys asking for help.
THE END?

ADITI SINGH

Aditi Singh is a student of 15 from Jharsuguda, Odisha. She is studies in standard 11th in DAV Public School. She has been writing since she was 13. She wants to pursue writing as her passion and career.

Insta id: Unspoken4583

SATAN'S LEGACY

When the world's on fire the lights would perish,

On the surface of abhorrence where no love'd
cherish.

When plants are croaked with leaves so old,

When the ground blazes till it turns gold.

When ravens replace the birds on trees,

When away from fire there's no end of hot breeze.

Paths that pave to heaven no more,

When the devil is the one whom the world adores.

When the hell is nowhere just within you,

The legacy you find coming up through.

Where death is not the escape from it,

Where envy wouldn't have assuaged even a bit.

When there's no care just the jealousy,

Is when you find the SATAN'S LEGACY.

BANUPRIYA K

She is K.Banupriya hails from Thoothukudi district. She is currently pursuing Second year post graduate Mathematics. She usually writes a blog. She got a medal for her service from Indian National Development and Reformation Association shortly abbreviated as INDRA TRUST.

Insta id : banu_k_11

LIGHT IN THE DARK!

The boy who lived sweetly in a lonely room in the
dark,

Suddenly came to the outside world.

To him who saw the light in the dark room,

The lighted world seemed dark.

He was afraid to see the languages and actions of
man.

He is afraid when the sun shines on him.

He sees the light of lightning and is afraid.

He hears the screams of thunder and is terrified.

He treats animals with love.

Speaks silently to them.

But when he sees humans, he runs away in fear
and hides.

There is no one to love

Even though there are so many human beings
around him.

This world was hell for him at that time.

DEBANJALI ADHIKARY

Debanjali Adhikary is a 19 year old girl, who lives in Delhi. She wants to be a doctor. She is a bengali girl. And an international author.

Insta id: Creationsoul7

THE HORROR NIGHT

When the lightning strikes.

A window opens and closes,

One puzzle one mansion,

Have heard or seen,

Away from the city in the rugged forests,

There is a haunt of ghosts in that mansion,

Hardly anyone has stayed in that mansion.

Some voices come from there,

When there is silence all around,

Has anyone seen some wandering shadows,

But he doesn't hurt anyone,

Don't scare anyone

Who wakes up when it's dark,

Yes-yes, I have also heard or seen it,

no one goes that way

The address of that mansion is not given.

One day big steps towards that mansion,

The rustle of the trees and the evening woke up a
headache,

The mansion was burnt to ashes,

His ashes were just achieved,

It was evening while returning,

The opposite foot ran to the house,

There is a mansion, that mansion.

SMITA G NAIDU

Smita naidu is a computer post graduate with double diploma, MCA, DCA, DISM, CPISM, this is her qualification, she is working as a business head of procode technologies, which is an IT company, she is also a writer, translator, transcriber, graphic designer, entrepreneur, Youtuber, recruiter, life coach and a podcaster. As a writer, she has published more than 500. plus quotes, which are visible on Google too, she has published a few books as coauthor too, and several are piled up, her solo book will also be published soon! She was also into forever book of world record recently, as an emerging entrepreneur.

Insta id: @keep_mind_and_body_healthy

I WILL KILL ALL MEN

He told me, that I was supposed to sacrifice since I was just a kid, as if I had no brain, no feelings, and was just a machine, I will kill him, and cut his brain for he should not have a mind of his own, I will chop his heart, and then he will just be a machine, Oh men, now better beware, for a woman is not your puppet anymore!

He told her, that he will drive her safely, to her home, but abused her instead, and took advantage of her trust, I will kill him, and make him dress like a woman, tie him hard, and thrash him, so that he understands her pain, oh men now better beware, for a woman is not weak anymore!

He told my friend, that she is her wife, and he would love and take care of her, but instead, he insulted and bashed her every day. I will bash him, and cut him to small pieces. I will kill him, oh men beware, for a woman is not your property anymore!

I will kill him!

I will kill you man if you be unjust to a woman!

I will kill you all men if you do anything wrong!

I will kill, I am watching, I am coming, I am coming to kill!

I will Kill!

DEEPALAKSHMI.S

She is S.Deepalakshmi, born in Pondicherry, India. She aspires to become a physician. She loves to write about the reality rather than Dwelling in fantasy. Apart from writing she has keen interest towards human psychology, food science and culinary.

Insta id : Deeps_here

THE DREADFUL END

It all began with the light flicker

And it seemed to be the blood licker !

Suddenly, it was the entry door

Made noise with the loud down pour!

All our efforts went on vain

Since it started its heavy rain !

We all sat with heroic brave

Nevertheless we know it was near the grave!

Some expected it to be the last

Few recollected the past !

It was him who knocked the door

The blood on the room washed the floor!

THE DREADFUL END

P. SAKTHI VEL

He was born in virudhunagar district. His name is P.Sakthi Vel. He was social activist and artist. He was well player in athletic and kho-kho sports. And he was NCC and NSS member of school days. And now he is pursuing BBA. And he wants to become police officer.

Insta id : @ps.vel_332

HORROR

O little one, My little one,

Come with me, Your life is done.

Forget the future, Forget the past.

Life is over: Breathe your last."

Some teeth long for ripping,

Gleaming wet from black dog gums.

So you keep your eyes closed at the end.

You don't want to see such a mouth up close.

Before the bite, before its oblivion

In the goring of your soft parts,

The speckled lips will curl back in a whinny of excitement.

You just know it."

Walls have ears. Doors have eyes.

Trees have voices. Beasts tell lies.

Beware the rain. Beware the snow.

Beware the man You think you know."

BALASIVANETHRI GANESAN

Balasivanethri Ganesan is from Salem, Tamilnadu. She did Undergraduate English Literature in Government Arts College for Women, Salem-8 and she is now pursuing M.A English Literature in Government College of Arts and Science, Salem-7. She has faith in her Will Power, Endeavour and Hardwork. She believes in her writings and she wants to fight for justice through her pen. Now she is writing short stories and poems.

Insta id : halcyon._.07

SPOOKY SECONDS!!!

I was alone that day. It rained heavily, and power was cut too. I was watching outside the window, it's terribly dark there. Plants and trees looked like figures. In that wild wind's touch they moved dismally. Usually I'm not scared of this, but it's a little scary. I heard a sound like someone murmuring behind me. I was so scared, I got more sweaty and my pulse was at its peak. I closed my eyes and held the rod of the window tightly. I convinced myself, it wouldn't be anyone there, it's all my imaginations. After a few seconds, I decided to turn and face whatever it is. Straight away I turned and slowly opened my one eye and I pacified and I unlocked my other eye. Rubbed my eyes and looked around. It was nothing and I felt calm. My stomach felt empty and I wanted to fill it, so I went to the kitchen. Droplet sound of the water leaking in the sink makes me a little frightful. I unbolt the tap and washed my hands. I felt someone breathing heavily behind me. That unknown person, held my shoulder, I shrieked and waked. It was a bad dream!

PRAGATI GIRI

She's Pragati Giri from UP state district Varanasi. She has done her graduation by B.Sc in biology stream where zoology is a core subject for her. Along with she's a Writer, Co-author for many Published E-books, Compiler, Guider, Educator, Sketcher etc. She is started her writing from her Childhood to adulthood. She likes to writes mostly thoughts, quotes, Aphorism, short stories, articles and sometimes poetries. Her dream is to be a published Author for her solo book & wants to become a civil servant for her nation. You can search her on/ IG Writing Acc: @writerpragati5409 IG Personal Acc: @__pragati_giri3 Tele: @Creativegir Blogger: pragatigiriwrites.blogspot.com/

Insta Id : @writerpragati5409

DREADFUL LAND

Don't you think, that is why we are now percepting our Earth is in dreadful and why we want to keep now in that species? Even only Earth is the planet where we can live as we want or without any doubts for food, for lives & with area to make house as we want to make to make a beautiful family even till third generation of family. How it's so amazing that we can live as on planet Earth? But we can't live like on another planets! But still we are calling our land or our Earth is 'Dreadful'. How shameful it's for us..? Cause, we can't live now on Earth as beautiful as we wanted to live, that's why it's calling dreadful by some peeps. All thing behind only we are...whether it comes to beautiful or dreadful..

NAVEEN BHARDWAJ

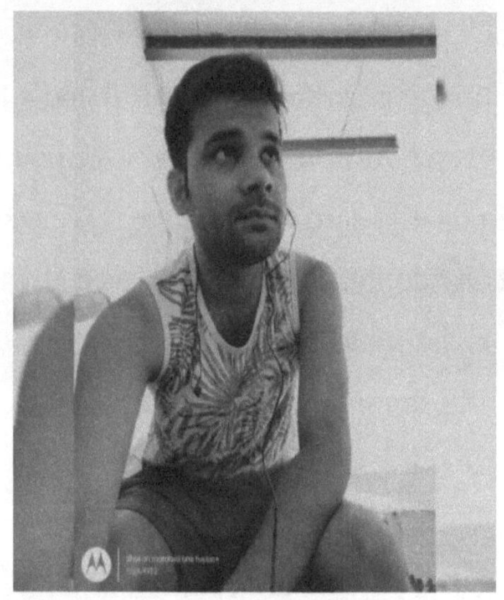

He is Naveen bhardwaj a programmer by profession a lover of poetry maker and like reading books and audiobooks and he has telegram channel @TheNBbook

Insta id : na.vin7832

HORROR

I am usually fascinated by horror stories in my life

When I was young my grandmother told me

Stories based on horror life;

Once there was a man where my grandmother
lived once;

There was a suspicious happened in that village

Where the man live alone;

The man woke up early and he finds some strange
voices;

The grandmother was strange as he had much
knowledge about this noises;

He told ram to close your window maybe there is
some bad soul roaming in a place;

Ram agreed by advice of her grandmother;

Her grandmother kept waited to see;

Finally Ram feel suffocated when the clock tick 3;

Her grandmother find out there some bad soul
drifting to the winds;

They call priest to get out the evil spirit;

They both get rid of those empty feeling;

DURGA BALAMADHAVAN

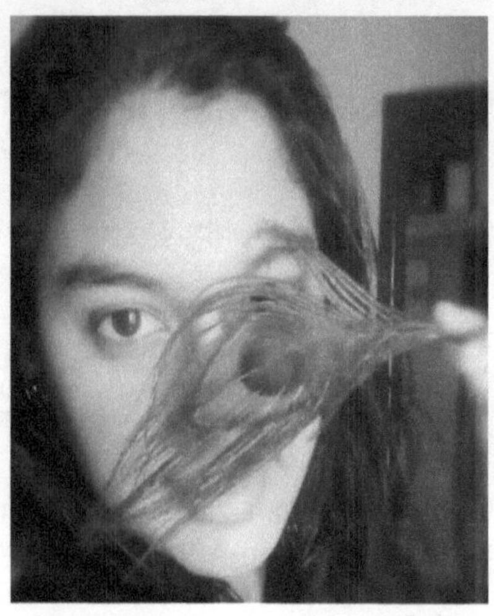

Durga Balamadhavan is a self-built writer & a 17 years old girl who has a kindling fire to achieve. She's a co-author of 40+ anthologies 3 world record anthologies till date & compiling her on going anthologies " The next billionaire" & "The Thirst to Travel". You can DM her in insta page @quotescumarts to get success & love quotes, poetry at a reasonable charge. Her soul finds happiness in Music, Dance, Creative Writing, Drawing & Painting...

Insta id : @quotescumarts, @uniquedreamerdurga

HORRIFYING BAD SPIRIT : Micro Tale

Two friends discussing the existence of ghost.

One believed while the other one opposed.

Suddenly, a terrifying voice with a creepy figure emerged telling "I'm here"

A few drops of fresh blood were dripping from the ceiling.

Lily's head turned up to the ceiling with a fastened heartbeat.

She noticed a gleaming mirror where a horrifying hand emerged pulling her into it.

Two friends went on a night ride in a hilly region.

It was mid night 3 am.

Though they were cautious on riding the bike,

A white figure crossed the road which made

Them to experience a dreadful mishap.

KRISHNAPRIYA

Krishnapriya from Thiruvattar. She is persuing her Master's degree in Arumanai. She is interested in writing verse, article, poems and short stories. She love to spend her time on reading novels.

Insta id : Krishna _jk_priya333

HORROR NIGHTS

Once a girl walking in the dark place,

Stranger man asking her to help please,

Nobodies near her to that dark town,

Stranger man slicely fainted down,

She is having some fear to help,

Stranger shows some money on his lap,

Her mind is striking on Seconds,

She starts to walk have mind to pretends,

Girl seen the stranger seems like her died father,

Stranger suddenly disguised himself ghost like horror,

Finally she wake-up and seen the mirror,

Oh no! it's my dream! dream! dream!

KAARTHIKVEL V.S

He is Kaarthikvel. He is a budding writer who loves to play with words.

Insta id: kavi_pithan05

IT WAS A NIGHT MARE

We were in the wild

She scared like a child

In the dense dark

We heard a dog's bark

Owls were flying

Trees were shaking

She holded my hands tightly

We stepped bravely

We took few steps behind

She scared because of the strong wind

As the time passes it becomes more darker

She became very afraid and hugged me tighter

It became very cold

But she felt warmth because of the hug she told

Suddenly I don't know where we were

I then realized that it was a night mare.

KEERTHANA

She is Keerthana. She wrote four anthologies and currently doing a compiler of a book. Her passions are photography and writing. Writing makes everyone new that the things that happen in her life too , writings makes her life into another world. Her native is tenkasi. "Be the person as the what you are " is the best thing of her.

Insta id : optimistic_keerthi

THE PHOTOFRAME

There was a room in our story. A doll which it have power to speak and doing some activities. It have a friend named gipsy. Gipsy is boy. Gipsy and a doll were lived in a room. They are doing fun always. One day they saw a portrait in a corner of a room. The portrait looks different from all other. They saw the portrait for a long time. Suddenly they entered in the portrait. There is big snow castle and a 2 warriors who they are not a live. Both are entering the castle. In each and every step they heared a song sound. Both are little scary. There is corner which it looks bright with a lamp. They were walking towards the lamp. Gipsy heard a sound and turn back. A rectail is eating the doll and then it turns as a ghost. Gipsy was scary and run a far... After he comes out from the castle he get back to his room. He saw his friend doll in his room as a big one. He went to touch the doll suddenly its gone. Gipsy get back from his dream. Then he realise the truth.

ABHINAV AGRAWAL

Abhinav Agrawal is a student of Allen Career Institute, Kota, Rajasthan, India. Having passed his 10th from the prestigious Sacred Heart School, Daltonganj. He now aspires to become a doctor. Since his childhood days he always had an inclination for writing poetry and other literary works. While at school he had participated in various poetry competitions and has also won at Kavyanjali 2019 national poetry writing competition. The lust for writing has always haunted him and he continues to compile poems. He has been a prolific reader and has been inspired by poets as Robert Frost, T. S. Eliot, Indian poets like Suryakant Tripathi 'Nirala', Mahadevi Verma, authors like JK Rowling. Recognizing this talent of his, his hindi teacher Mrs. Anupama Tiwari constantly encouraged him and thus the journey is on. His parents have also constantly been his support in this journey of his.

Insta id : @poem_parade and @itz_abhinav_0181

A TRIP TO HELL

I fell and fell and never stopped,

Into hell I think I dropped,

With so many dead souls it was topped,

I saw Cerberus after seeing me he gawped.

It was something I had never seen,

The Isle of Blest couldn't be left unseen,

I trudged forward, I got so keen,

I saw Hades and Persephone who was the queen.

The black horrifying Palace shook with roar,

I went forward for I wanted Tartarus to explore,

But Hades saw me, a deadly expression he wore,

I woke up in Fright and couldn't explore.

MUTHU VINNARASI M

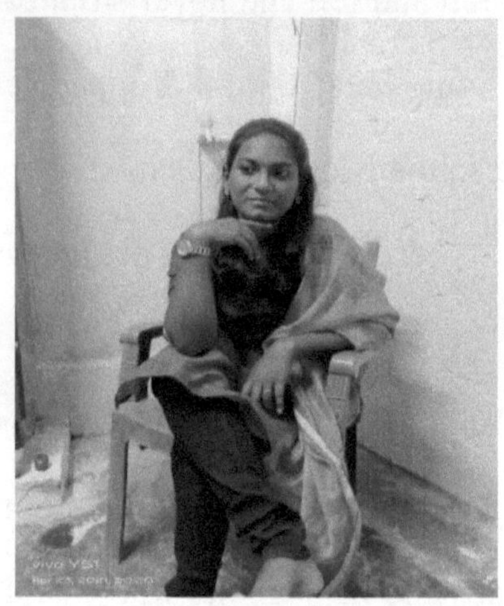

She is Muthu vinnarasi from Tamilnadu. She is a B.E graduate and now she is working in Banglore. She likes to share her thought through her writing.

Inst aid : Vinnarasi6999

AFTER DEATH

We would always wonder after death, were will we go.. I am now 21years old. Still I am not satisfied of most answers. And today I am going to let you know my father's reply for this question? We all people are living because of respiratory, digestion and excretion. The death is just stopping of functions of organs. In this world of living beings, there were one sense living being to six sense living being. We all having functions inside our body. So there is no outer reaction after death. Everything would have happen inside. Death is from inside.

I.K.HEMILAA

Hemilaa, a girl of 25 completed her master degree in English literature. Born in kovilpatti. A girl with dream become women with vision. She loves to write quotes, article stories. She is a lionhearted girl, wish to be " Hemilaa". " love is a key to success Spread love to everyone" Hemilaa

Insta id : Hemilaa_

SCARY NIGHT

Sometimes I walk at night alone

Someone follows me always

One day night I was sleeping in room

Someone knocks my door

I was wake up from the bed

When I open my door no one is there

I was scared

I just close all the door let no one in

Switch off all the lights

I don't want to see anything

The dark in my prison

This is my hell

Let block those sound

Life will be along

But still I'm hearing that sound

It's never leave me alone.

THE DREADFUL LAND